COMING TO CANADA

THE CHINESE

Annie Thomas

Weigl

Published by Weigl Educational Publishers Limited
6325 10th Street SE
Calgary, AB T2H 2Z9

Website: www.weigl.ca

Library and Archives Canada Cataloguing in Publication

Thomas, Annie, 1962-, author
      The Chinese / Annie Thomas.

(Coming to Canada)
Includes index.
Issued in print and electronic formats.
ISBN 978-1-4872-0161-6 (bound).--ISBN 978-1-4872-0162-3 (pbk.).--
ISBN 978-1-4872-0163-0 (epub)

      1. Chinese Canadians--History--Juvenile literature. 2. Chinese--
Canada--History--Juvenile literature. I. Title.

FC106.C5T46 2014   j971'.004951   C2014-904829-7
                                                C2014-904830-0

Printed in the United States of America in North Mankato, Minnesota
1 2 3 4 5 6 7 8 9 0 18 17 16 15 14

072014
WEP110614

Project Coordinator: Katie Gillespie
Art Director: Terry Paulhus

We acknowledge the financial support of the Government of Canada through
the Canada Book Fund for our publishing activities.

CONTENTS

INTRODUCING THE CHINESE

In 1788, Captain John Meares, a British fur trader, brought 50 men from China to Canada. They landed on Vancouver Island in the northwest. The men were **smiths** and carpenters and were very hard workers. They helped Captain Meares build a trading post, including a fortress and a dockyard. They also helped him build a **schooner**. Captain Meares was so impressed with their work that he brought another 70 men from China the following year. Then, there was no written record of the Chinese in Canada for almost 70 years. The next group of Chinese **immigrants** to arrive in Canada came when gold was discovered. After that, they came when the construction of the Canadian Pacific Railway began.

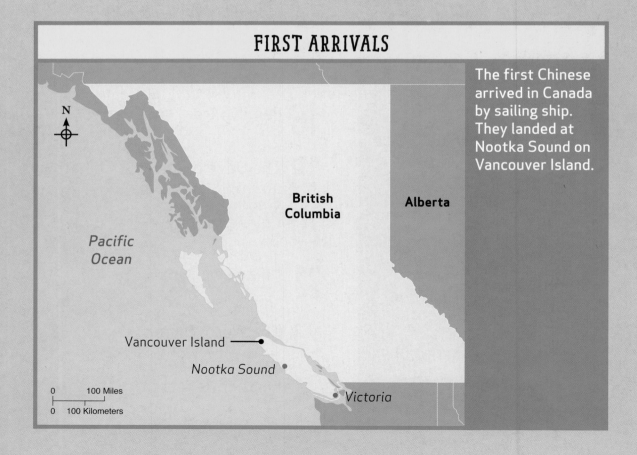

FIRST ARRIVALS

The first Chinese arrived in Canada by sailing ship. They landed at Nootka Sound on Vancouver Island.

N

British Columbia

Alberta

Pacific Ocean

Vancouver Island

Nootka Sound

Victoria

0   100 Miles

0   100 Kilometers

The Chinese were recruited by Captain John Meares to help with a trade relationship between Guangzhou, China, and Canada. Meares wanted to trade sea otter skins.

Between 1788 and 1789, **120** Chinese men arrived in Canada.

Today, **more than 1.3 million** Chinese live in Canada.

THE SPANISH INVASION

In 1789, the Spanish arrived at Nootka Sound, Vancouver Island, and took **possession** of it. They drove out the British, including Captain Meares and his Chinese workers. No one knows exactly what happened to the Chinese. It is thought that some may have been sent back to China, some may have escaped, and some may have been killed.

THE NEXT WAVE OF IMMIGRANTS

In 1857, gold was found in the Fraser Valley, British Columbia. Thousands of miners, including many Chinese, flocked to the area to make their fortune. Many of the Chinese came by boat from San Francisco and travelled through Victoria to reach the Fraser Valley. Most of these men came from an area called Guangzhou (Canton) in South China and from Hong Kong. The Chinese labourers worked hard so that they could send money home. The women stayed at home to care for their families and uphold family traditions. Life was often harsh for Chinese immigrants.

The town of Yale was founded in 1848 as a result of the gold rush. It is located in the Fraser Valley.

Gold could be found in river beds. Once the sand and gravel was washed away, the gold was left behind.

CHINA IN THE MID-19TH CENTURY

People faced many problems in the **province** of Guangdong during the 19th century. The population had grown so quickly that there was great pressure on resources, such as food. In the 1850s, there was a peasant **rebellion**. This rebellion claimed many lives and forced several men to **emigrate** to find work.

THE CANADIAN PACIFIC RAILWAY

Between 1880 and 1885, about 17,000 Chinese arrived in Canada. During this time, most of the Chinese population was employed to help build the Canadian Pacific Railway. The railway was built to link the eastern parts of Canada with British Columbia in the west. There was a great deal of opposition to using Chinese labour. **Petitions** were organized against the Chinese. However, Prime Minister John A. Macdonald insisted that without employing Chinese labourers, there would be no railway.

On July 4, 1886, the first train arrived in the west. From that time on, regular trains ran from the east to the west.

Conditions were harsh for Chinese workers. They were given the dangerous task of tunnel blasting. Hundreds died from drowning, freezing, **exhaustion**, or tunnels collapsing. They were paid $1 per day, which was less than half the wage of other workers. Despite the problems they faced, the Chinese were known as capable, hard workers.

The phrase, "A Chinaman's chance," referred to the harsh conditions faced by the Chinese workers and the chances they had to take to get their jobs done.

Andrew Onderdonk was the engineer in charge of the dangerous section of the railway that most Chinese worked on. He said that six Chinese workers died for every 1 mile (1.6 kilometres) of track that was laid.

HEAD TAX

After the building of the railway was finished, many Canadians, especially those in British Columbia, wanted to stop Chinese immigration. In 1885, a "head tax" was introduced for every Chinese immigrant. The Chinese were the only **ethnic** group required to pay a tax to enter Canada. The tax was set at $50 for Chinese immigrants, but was just $25 for British immigrants. In 1901, the tax was increased to $100, and increased again in 1903 to $500. Although it was very difficult for the Chinese to pay this amount of money, they still came to Canada. The chances of finding work were better than they were in China. However, in most cases, the men came alone. The high cost of the head tax meant they could not afford to bring their wives and children with them.

Some descendants of people who paid the Chinese head tax work hard to ensure that their stories are told. Debbie Yam, whose grandfather was issued a head tax certificate, visits schools to speak about the issue.

In **China**, a labourer could earn **$2 per month.** In **Canada**, the same labourer could earn between **$20** and **$40** per month.

Some Chinese immigrants found work in Canada's agricultural industry. They performed outdoor labour, such as harvesting lettuce crops.

IMMIGRATION IN THE 20TH CENTURY

Although the Chinese had risked their lives to help build the Canadian Pacific Railway, they found that they were no longer welcome by the Canadian government in the late 1800s and early 1900s. Some of these men returned to China, but many stayed in Canada. Some took on jobs that other Canadians did not want, such as cooking and cleaning. Others set up their own businesses. Gradually, the Chinese built strong communities in urban areas. As immigration began to increase in the second half of the 20th century, these areas attracted more and more Chinese. These communities came to be known as "Chinatowns." Chinatowns grew in many Canadian cities. Today, these areas are an important part of city life.

The town of Chemainus, British Columbia celebrates its rich history with more than 40 large-scale murals. *Memories of a Chinese Boy* by Cheng Shu-Ren features a store operated by Ning Chang, the first Chinese child born in Chemainus.

STOP IMMIGRATION!

On July 1, 1923, Canada passed the Chinese Exclusion Act. This stopped almost all Chinese immigration. The act was not **repealed** until 1947. Between 1923 and 1947, there were less than 50 Chinese immigrants allowed into the country. Chinese Canadians found this law **humiliating**. They called the day that the act was passed, "Humiliation Day." They closed their shops and refused to celebrate Canada Day.

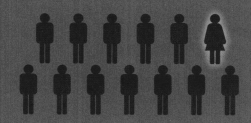

By **1931**, the population of Chinese in Canada was about **45,000**. Of this, only about **3,500** were women.

In 2006, Prime Minister Stephen Harper formally apologized to the Chinese Canadian community. Those who had paid the head tax were awarded $20,000 in compensation.

REFUGEES

Many Chinese people have come to Canada as **refugees**. World War II (1939–1945) and the Cultural Revolution in China (1965–1968) are two events that have forced people to flee their hometowns. When Hong Kong was invaded by Japan in 1941, many Chinese people fled to mainland China and to countries such as Canada, who were **allies** of the British. During the 1960s, the Cultural Revolution in China caused disruption throughout the country. The revolution became violent and food became scarce, forcing people to leave.

ADRIENNE CLARKSON

Adrienne Clarkson came to Canada in 1942, at the age of three. She and her family were refugees from Hong Kong. After attending university, she became a journalist and television presenter. In 1999, she became the 26th governor general of Canada. She was Canada's first governor general of Asian origin.

ELLEN FAIRCLOUGH

Ellen Fairclough was the first woman to become a federal cabinet minister. She was the minister of citizenship and immigration from 1958 to 1962. She was successful in increasing the number of immigrants allowed into Canada and introducing a more **liberal** policy on refugees.

From 1978 to 1981, Vietnamese Chinese refugees arrived in Canada. They were fleeing a country that had been devastated by the Vietnam War (1965–1975). Although the war was over, the country was still suffering from a lack of freedom and a fear of the **communist** government. Despite earlier moves towards **integration** of immigrants, many Canadians were unhappy about their arrival.

THE POINTS SYSTEM

In 1967, Canada began using a points system for immigrants. Points were awarded for things such as age, education, special skills, and a job offer. This system was not concerned with where the person came from, but only whether or not a person would be a good Canadian citizen. The system is still used for people wanting to move to Canada today.

At the end of the Vietnam War, many Vietnamese Chinese people fled the country by sea.

FAMILY LIFE

In the 1800s and the first half of the 1900s, there was very little family life for Chinese Canadians. The men had left their wives and families at home to find work in Canada. This changed after the Chinese Exclusion Act was repealed and more Chinese immigrants, including women and children, arrived in Canada. Areas that had previously been regarded as "slums," grew into neighbourhoods where family life and businesses thrived. All through this time, cultural traditions remained important to the Chinese population. Family **hierarchy** was still observed. Extended families lived together and people took care of their elders. Many people attended Chinese temples and Chinese theatres became popular.

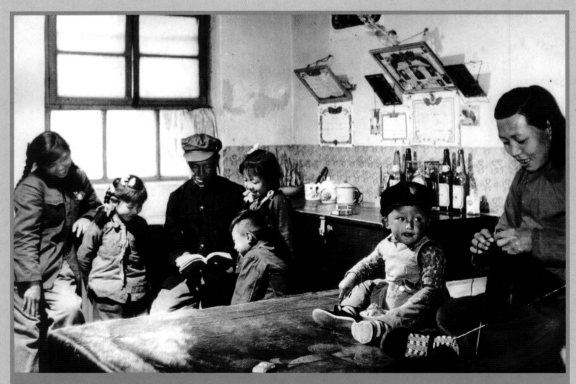

Family values have always been important to the Chinese. They maintained these values even when they emigrated to a new country.

Getting married and having children was very important to Chinese in rural China, as this meant families would have workers for their land. Marriage is still an important Chinese tradition today.

In the late 1920s, it is estimated that there were only about **10 married Chinese women** in Canada.

THE DEVELOPMENT OF CHINATOWNS

In the late 1800s and early 1900s, Chinese communities were largely viewed as overcrowded slums. However, in 1947, two important events led to a growth of confidence in these communities. The Chinese Exclusion Act was repealed and Chinese people gained back the right to vote. They had not been able to vote since 1875. These events changed life for the Chinese population in Canada. Immigration grew, employment opportunities increased, land was bought, and many new businesses opened up.

The entrance to Chinatown in Victoria, British Columbia, was built in 1981. During festivals, it is decorated with red lanterns.

Today, "old" Chinatown and "new" Chinatown exist side by side in many places. In Victoria, for example, there are old narrow alleyways that date back to the early 1900s. Beside these alleyways are wide new streets with brightly coloured buildings and decorative calligraphy.

Many Chinese businessmen have invested in the upgrade of Chinatowns. They have made sure that these areas remain an important part of Chinese Canadian history. They are also an important part of the urban landscape in many cities, such as Vancouver and Calgary.

Some Chinese view the old areas of Chinatowns as representing conflicts of the past. However, many others see them as places where Chinese culture has been preserved and is respected.

THE FIRST CHINATOWN

Victoria, British Columbia, was the first destination for many Chinese immigrants. This is where Canada's first Chinatown grew. As well as the miners and labourers who came to seek work in the goldfields and on the railroad, shopkeepers such as barbers, cobblers, and tailors opened stores to provide services for these workers. Living conditions were poor at this time. There was no running water and accommodations were crowded.
The Chinatowns of the late 1800s and early 1900s were very different from the Chinatowns of today.

CHINESE TODAY

In 1967, the federal government introduced a new immigration policy. This policy identified potential immigrants by their country of residence, rather than by their ethnicity. This meant that people of Chinese origin from countries other than China were able to immigrate. Many professional and skilled Chinese workers from all over the world moved to Canada.

By the late 1980s, the Chinese had been officially recognized by the government for their contributions to Canada. Today, there are Chinese workers in all areas of Canada's workforce. They are represented in the arts, sciences, sports, and in professions such as law and medicine. They work in community services and there are many **entrepreneurs**.

Today, Chinese Canadians make up about 4% of Canada's total population. Chinese Canadians still have strong ties to their cultural background. Their customs and beliefs are a very important part of daily life.

Patrick Chan is a Canadian figure skating champion of Chinese descent. Chan won two silver medals at the 2014 Olympic Winter Games in Sochi, Russia.

CHINESE NEW YEAR

One of the most important traditional celebrations is Chinese New Year. It is the longest Chinese holiday of the year. Many symbols associated with Chinese New Year are red. It is believed that the colour red prevents bad luck. People dress in red clothes and many Chinese New Year decorations are red.

Parades are held where people wear costumes and a dragon marches down the street. The dragon is a loved symbol of China. It is believed to bring rain for crops, and to scare away evil spirits. Drums beat and dances are performed. It is a happy time of celebration for Chinese people all over the world.

In 2011, there were about *800,000* Chinese language speakers. Chinese is Canada's **third most common** spoken language after English and French.

CHINESE QUIZ

1 In which year did the first Chinese immigrants arrive in Canada?

2 How many Chinese arrived in Canada to help build the Canadian Pacific Railway?

3 How much was the Chinese head tax when it was first introduced?

4 Which world event forced people to move to Canada as refugees in the early 1940s?

5 On what date was the Chinese Exclusion Act passed?

6 Who was Canada's first governor general of Asian origin?

7 In which year was the points system introduced?

8 What did Patrick Chan win at the 2014 Olympic Winter Games?

9 Where was Canada's first Chinatown?

10 About how many Chinese people live in Canada today?

Answers
1. 1788
2. about 17,000
3. $50
4. World War II
5. July 1, 1923
6. Adrienne Clarkson
7. 1967
8. two silver medals
9. Victoria, British Columbia
10. more than 1.3 million

KEY WORDS

allies: individuals or countries that have officially agreed to give help and support to another

communist: a political system based on collective ownership of property

emigrate: to leave one's own country to settle permanently in another country

entrepreneurs: people who organize and control businesses that may have involved a certain risk to set up and operate

ethnic: relating to a group of people who share the same customs, religion, culture, and language

exhaustion: to be completely tired out to the point of having very little energy

hierarchy: a group of people organized by rank, one above the other

humiliating: causing a person to feel ashamed by hurting his or her self-respect and dignity

immigrants: people who have come to live in another country permanently

integration: the bringing together of people of different ethnic groups

liberal: to be less strict

petitions: formal documents, signed by one or more people, asking an authority for a particular right or benefit

possession: to take control of

province: a territory outside a country, but under control of that country

rebellion: an organized resistance to an authority, such as a government

refugees: people taking shelter, especially in a foreign country, from war or oppression

repealed: revoked or officially withdrawn

schooner: a sailing boat that has two or more masts

smiths: labourers who work in metal, such as iron

INDEX

FURTHER RESEARCH

Many books and websites provide information about the Chinese. To learn more about this topic, borrow books from the library, or search the internet. Check out some of the following websites to discover more interesting facts about the Chinese.

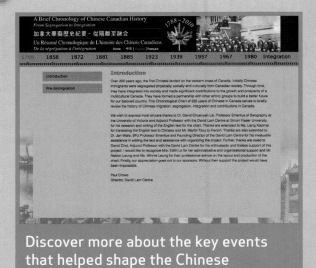

Discover more about the key events that helped shape the Chinese Canadian experience at: www.sfu.ca/chinese-canadian-history/chart_en.html

Learn more about the history of Chinese immigrants in British Columbia at: www.library.ubc.ca/chineseinbc/

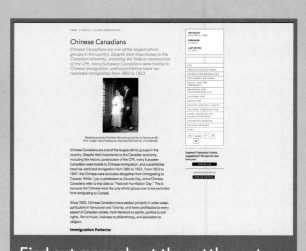

Find out more about the settlement patterns of early Chinese immigrants at: www.thecanadianencyclopedia.ca/en/article/chinese-canadians/